This Book Belongs To:

....

....

Clumsy Shoofully at the Beach

Written and Published By: Sunshine Creations

Illustrated By: Ali Pourazar

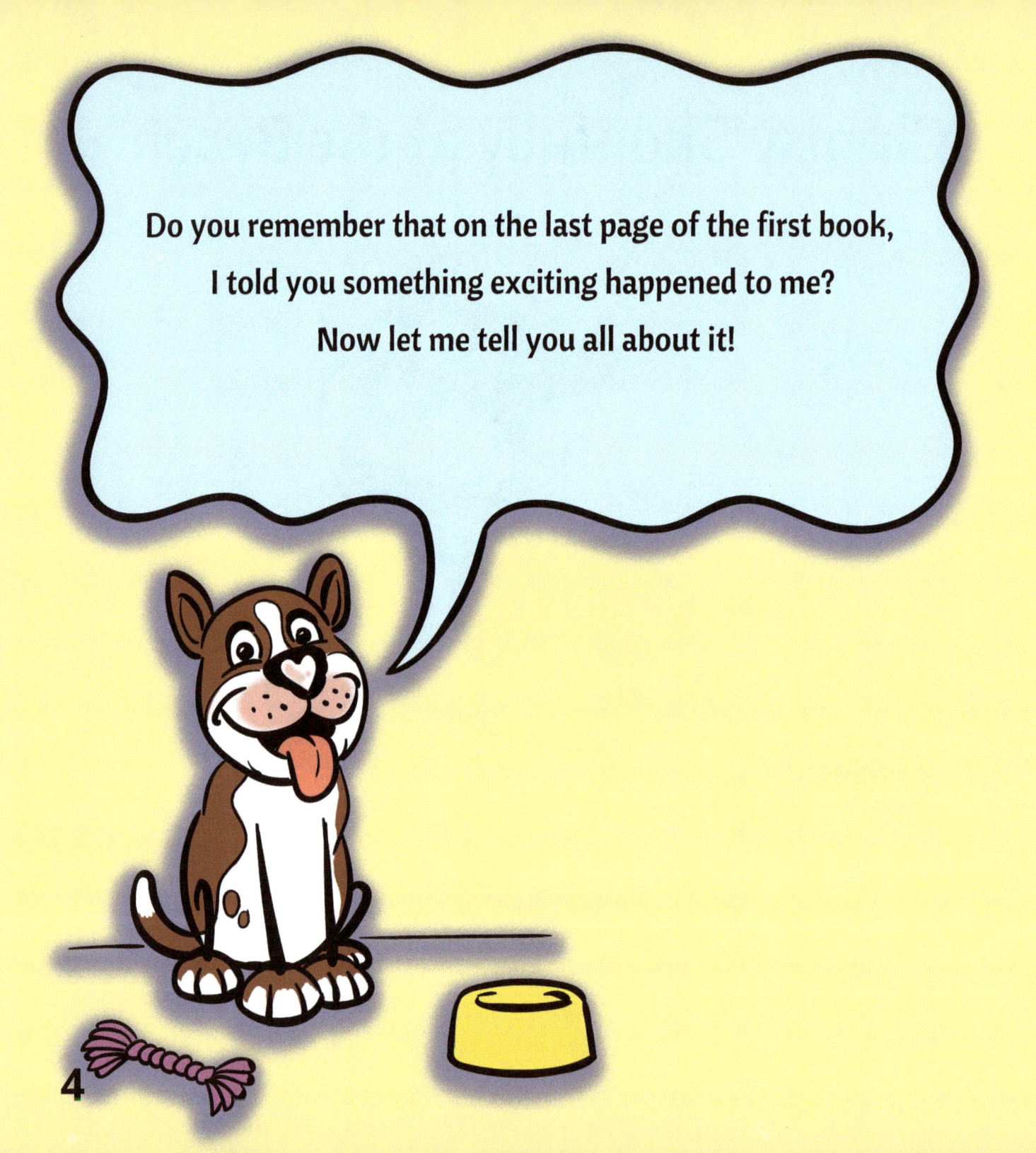

One day, a different family came to our house. They were also humans. They talked to our humans and laughed a lot. There was a woman who I think was a mommy, there was a daddy and then there was a little boy!

The little boy ran towards our box and started staring at me and my siblings. His eyes were shining, and he seemed excited.

Suddenly, he reached into the box and grabbed me! He smelled good and he was so gentle with me! I gave him a lick on his nose and right after he yelled:
"I want this one", "I want this one".

As he was holding me and I was busy wagging my tail and licking his hands, I think I peed a tiny bit on his shoes! Oops! I thought he might get mad, but he started laughing and kissing me!

It was sweet! I thought if we can laugh together at good things and bad things, we obviously belong to each other! My heart was full of joy, and I think his was too.

My new family gave me some time to say goodbye to my mommy and siblings. I licked all of them. Mommy told me to be a good boy and spread love and kindness wherever I go! I will never forget mommy's advice.

Let me tell you something, he might seem young, but he knows very well how to pet me. His hands were scratching my head and the car was moving, It felt so good. I could barely keep my eyes open!

Then the car stopped, and the boy's parents told "Ben" to get out of the car! Hmmm, so my new friend's name is Ben! I like Ben! Ben gently hugged me, and we got out of the car.

The new mommy said: "I wonder if Shoofully likes the ocean!".

I thought to myself:

What is the ocean?
Who is the ocean?
Can I eat the ocean?

Soon I found out that the ocean is a giant body of water. Water was everywhere. It was blue and beautiful, and did I say, giant? It had waves and waves made loud noises.

Then I realized, we are walking on the beach! If you don't know, the beach is just next to the ocean! It's full of soft tiny things called sand or sometimes it has huge rocks.

There was so much to take in and it got me really excited. So, I kept barking and wagging my tail. Ben had to eventually put me down. I think he was nervous to let go of me, but I'm a smart boy! I know to stay close to him.

Once I felt the soft sand under my paws, I thought I should taste it! Let me tell you, it doesn't taste good!

I looked at Ben and then started running. I wanted Ben to chase me, and he did. He is fast and also a good playmate.

I ran left and right. I fell on my face a couple of times, but I wasn't hurt

I even ran down to the water and jumped in! OK, almost. The water was big and loud, and I was a little bit afraid at first but then I got used to it. I'm still very careful though. I don't go too deep, and I always stay close to Ben!

When we both got tired of running, I started digging holes in the sand. I don't even know where the idea came from, I just knew that I liked doing it.

Ben started laughing and took pictures of me! Am I a super star now? Who knows!

I had a lot of sand in my fuzzy fur, and I was a bit wet. Ben's mom said, "let's go home and clean up this cutie!".

Check us out in Instagram and Facebook:

 Facebook.com/sunshinecreations555

 Instegram.com/sunshinecreations555

Email us at: sunshinecreations555@Gmail.com

Check out book #1 in my Amazon author page

amazon.com/author/sunshinecreations555

www.ingramcontent.com/pod-product-compliance
Lightning Source LLC
Chambersburg PA
CBHW051306110526
44589CB00025B/2957